straight talk
from a
Brethren
sister

Wanda L. Callahan
Foreword by Earle W. Fike Jr.

Herald
Press

Scottdale, Pennsylvania
Waterloo, Ontario

Library of Congress Cataloguing-in-Publication Data
Callahan, Wanda L., 1924-
    Straight talk from a Brethren sister / Wanda L. Callahan.
      p. cm.
    ISBN 0-8361-9130-7 (alk. paper)
    1. Callahan, Wanda L., 1924- I. Title

    BX7843.C34 A3 2000
    248.4'865—dc21   00-022508

The paper used in this publication is recycled and meets the min-
imum requirements of American National Standard for
Information Sciences—Permanence of Paper for Printed Library
Materials, ANSI Z39.48-1984.

STRAIGHT TALK FROM A BRETHREN SISTER
Copyright © 2000 by Herald Press, Scottdale, Pa. 15683
      Published simultaneously in Canada by Herald Press,
      Waterloo, Ont. N2L 6H7. All rights reserved
Library of Congress Catalog Number: 00-022508
International Standard Book Number: 0-8361-9130-7
Printed in the United States of America
Book design by Gwen M. Stamm, Herald Press, in collaboration
with Michael A. King, Pandora Press U.S.
Cover design by Gwen M. Stamm, Herald Press

10 09 08 07 06 05 04 03 02 01 00   10 9 8 7 6 5 4 3 2 1

To order or request information, please call
1-800-759-4447 (individuals); 1-800-245-7894 (trade)
Website: www.mph.org

*In honor
of Monroe Miller and
with thanksgiving
for my Brethren heritage.*

Contents

Foreword

IF YOU EXPECTED *STRAIGHT TALK* to be a catchy title unconnected to the content of Wanda's book, you'd be wrong. She is direct, unblinking, often confrontational in her witness to what she believes is the good news. And her voice comes to us from a life pilgrimage in service and ministry which gives authenticity to her "talk."

Anabaptists will find their hearts warmed by her basic stance on peace; her affirmations about caring for the "least of these" among us; embracing not only the poor but those incarcerated, some of whom are on death row. Anabaptists will be both comforted and cheered by her commitment to "live in keeping with the spirit and teachings of Jesus."

Persons like me, who have a streak of pietism running on a parallel track with our Anabaptist genes, will rejoice in her understanding of New Testament acceptance of those with whom we differ; her strong convictions about the importance of community; her undeveloped but simple understanding of life after death for the Christian; and her concern for the whole person, including spirit and body, manifested in an evangelistic style which includes both the Word that saves and acts of service and ministry which incarnate the Word.

At many places in her book I say "Amen." But at places I join with those who, across the years, have distressed her with "Yes buts!" I do find her prophetic stance to be strong. Her pastoral care for the underprivileged and dispossessed is more exemplary than I can manage in my own life. Of course that's not so much a "Yes but" as a needed challenge.

Yet in her own straight talk style, I fear Wanda is plagued with a Brethren virus. The symptoms are being more tolerant and accepting of the poor than the rich; more encouraging to the "down and out" than the "up and out." She seemed simply to judge and write off the "well-to-do ladies" who brought "rich" gifts to the children. They were denied future charitable efforts with the children without receiving pastoral care or efforts to help them understand how they could respond more helpfully. The store owner with the disgusting sign was summarily rejected as self-righteous and deaf.

It also disappoints me that Wanda sometimes dismisses parishioners who have said "Yes but" by saying their "Yes buts" don't really bother her. If she means they will not deter her from serving in a way she believes consistent with the New Testament Christ, then I approve. If she means she doesn't really care what they say, then that seems in opposition to her own strong belief about acceptance in the community of faith which is the body of Christ.

But then prophets are not supposed to be graduates of the school of "How to Win Friends and Influence People." They are commissioned to confront those at ease in Zion and to comfort those in distress in Zion. Whichever we readers are, Wanda's straight talk has something for us. If we say "Yes but," she may smile, say "What else is new?" and continue a ministry that sparkles with risk and service.

—*Earle W. Fike Jr.*
Pastor Emeritus, Church of the Brethren

Author's Preface

I HAD A BIRTHDAY RECENTLY. It was my seventy-fourth. Birthdays are always a time to look back, especially when the years begin to pile up. Perhaps as one gets older, looking ahead tends to make you frown, thinking of what may be ahead as you get even more creaky with every passing year.

Looking back, I am struck by two things. First, there is the diversity. I certainly have managed to get involved in a lot of stuff. Everything from teaching to preaching, from art to nature study, from government to social work, from travel to gardening, and especially from conflict to peacemaking.

That brings me to the second part of my discovery. There is the fact that as a bona fide pacifist, I seem often to be in the thick of things that cause conflict.

This book is called *Straight Talk from a Brethren Sister*, but the "straight talk" I originally had in mind was rooted in reflecting on how often my resistance to "Yes but" has been what has seemed to plunge me into conflict. "Yes," people say, "that's good or right or possible, *but. . . .*" Then they go on to explain why it is not feasible there and in that situation. So there I am, professing pacifism, yet finding myself once more in the thick of conflict.

My befuddlement has to do with the fact that, as a Christian pastor, most of my contacts are with other Christians. The root of most of my ideas and actions seem to me to be based on Christ. Why then should there ever be any conflict?

I'd like to share with you some of the places of conflict. See what you think about why this happens.

—*Wanda Callahan*
Wawaka, Indiana

straight talk
from a
Brethren
sister

1

Living Simply

Now I realize that my work with death row inmates falls into the area that is controversial. We'll talk more about that later, but surely an idea like simple living is nothing to stir anyone up. Not so, I found out.

When our youngest son finished his first year of college, my husband and I both quit our jobs, sold our house, and went into Brethren Volunteer Service. The letters, visits, and calls we got covered the whole array of advice. We heard from people who were seriously worried about us. We heard from people who scolded us like we were little children. Didn't we realize how old we were? (I was fifty-four and my husband sixty.) Didn't we realize that we might get sick? The world had enough irresponsible people in it, did we have to join them?

Most people, however, just kept reminding us that we spent plenty of time doing various service projects for the church, for the school, and for the community. We didn't have to go away from home. There were plenty of ways to serve, right in Goshen.

Of course, they were right about that, but in reality, they were missing the point entirely. We owned a nine-room house and lots of stuff in it that made it a very comfortable and beautiful home. That home and the fact that we were giving it up was the point of contention for most of our adversaries. "Are you crazy? Don't sell your home. What are you going to come back to? Your boys grew up here, you need to save it for them."

We tried to explain that we had reached a place where we no longer owned the house, but rather, it owned us. We told people it was a struggle to keep the home as we felt it should be kept.

For example, the house was two-and-a-half stories tall, with forty-some windows that always needed to be washed and to have screens or storm windows put up. The eave troughs, way up there, were always full of maple seeds or maple leaves that had to be cleaned out.

We bought the house in 1955 and sold it in 1978. During that time we were constantly refurbishing it or remodeling it. When I tried politely to say these things to my friends, in-laws, and various other assorted people, I got the "Yes buts" thick and fast. Yes, but you'll be sorry. Yes, but you just can't give up what you have worked so hard for.

When we tried softly to remind these people that Jesus said, "Put the kingdom first, and all the things you need will be added unto you," we got an earful!

One good friend, a strong leader in the church, never really forgave me. Being a believer in Christ, she said, didn't give me the right to be stupid. What was I going to do, she asked, just sit down and wait for God to take care of me?

Of course, she believed you could pray to God for help, but you were also supposed to help yourself. It said that in the Bible, she was sure, but she couldn't show me where. In 1992 when my husband died of cancer and I was left feeling pretty destitute, this same friend took it on herself to very emphatically remind me of all this.

How could these people get so worked up about this when, basically, it was none of their business? If they knew my husband and me at all, they knew we would never come to them for help, even if we ended up totally destitute.

Perhaps our willingness to give up almost everything made them feel bad as followers of Christ. We never once said, or even thought, that others should do what we were doing. But the message that we were passing judgment on others came through loud and clear. If we felt it was wrong for us to relish our possessions and hang on to them, then we must also think it was wrong for others.

As I have grown older and more fundamental in my religion, realization has come. It was just Satan speaking through them, making a last-ditch effort to stop us from making a move that would change everyday for the rest of our lives.

There was never any real danger that our mission would be scrapped, but believe me, there were some real moments of turmoil. Every doubt anyone presented revisited a doubt that we had already thought of, talked about, and put aside.

The economy was depressed at the time we sold our house, so we knew the price we received would not be high. We also decided to sell it to the local Mennonite church for one of their large refugee families from Vietnam. We knew they couldn't afford to pay a high price. We decided also to give them most of the contents of the house. New appliances, whole rooms full of furniture, many things with many memories attached, were left behind.

Two painful memories from this part of the transition remain. First, just a few weeks after we gave all of these household things to one family, we found they were selling them to other refugees for high prices.

Second, I had to go through all those drawers and cupboards; the cellar, attic, and garage; sorting out things. I did this by sitting down before each place with four boxes—one box that would be thrown away, one that would be given away to various people, one that would be sold at a garage sale, and one we would keep. A lot of tears fell into those boxes, but there were also a lot of smiles, as we remembered all kind of things from our then thirty-three years of marriage.

That block of time set the course for many other decisions in our life. Almost always, the same sort of thing happened. Someone always thought it was foolish, or dangerous, or at the very least, too far-out to be sensible. We had heard the same negative reaction when we adopted our boys years before.

I went through this most recently two-and-a-half years ago. On my seventy-second birthday, I decided to leave the old peoples home where I had lived for nine years. It was a good safe place to be while my husband went through his last stages of cancer, but I was needed at a church that was having trouble. My money supply was short, so why not go? Again, the "Yes buts" came pouring in. Again, I went anyway, knee-deep in doubts, but the doubts were not strong enough to make me forget that when I followed Christ, ever and always, everything I needed was provided.

If my life is to be any kind of example, then I guess we can always know that following Christ is always going to be tough. This is not because God's promises are not there for us. They are. They are emphatically.

No, it's tough because the world and often the people you love the most are going to try their best to block your way. They will be doing this for your own good, of course. So you must keep on loving them, even while you politely keep on doing what you feel Christ is leading you to do.

2

The Value
of Each One

As I LOOK BACK OVER MY LIFE, it is easy to see that I have spent a great amount of time trying to explain one group of people to another group. Because I work with the poor, the prisoners, the afflicted, and all kinds of cast out people, I have to explain to them why the good people of the church are so willing to put them aside. Because I work in the church with church people, I have to explain that God loves the cast out—the poor, the prisoners, the afflicted. I've been at this for at least fifty years, and I'm almost certain that most of my effort has been wasted.

It seems that we can't quite reach the place where we can say,

As God will not stop loving me,
I cannot stop loving you.
As God forgives me—I forgive you.
As God accepts me—I accept you.

Instead, we practice conditional love. I'm a Christian so of course I love you but. . . . Or I'd love everyone if. . . . Or I'll love you when. . . . We attach all kinds of stipulations to our statements of love.

Many people in our world are desperate. They find little solace in the church or among its people because, as God's representatives, people in the church too often show a harsh and judgmental side to the needy. The ones who are hurting look elsewhere—to the bottle, the needle, or other life-destroying actions. Isn't that strange because after Jesus came, there was new hope for those who fail?

Do you remember the story of the woman who was dragged before Jesus by men anxious to stone her to death? After he had dispersed the men, Jesus told the woman, "I find no fault with you."

He gave the judgment back to her. He saw her as a real person, not just as a perpetuator of sin. He saw her in her worst moment as someone valuable, someone who could be responsible for herself. Christ never gives up on us.

Many times in the New Testament, Jesus is said to have compassion on someone—the sick of all kinds, the 5,000 people on the hillside who were hungry, the children, people like Zacchaeus who were outcasts because of their professions, the lepers, and people of ill repute such as this woman.

What does compassion mean? It doesn't just mean sympathy. Let me give you an example that points out the difference between compassion and sympathy. When I was teaching special education, a well-to-do women's club wanted to come to my class to put on parties for the children several times a year at special holidays. It seemed that would be okay, but it wasn't.

These were twenty little kids from ages five to ten with mental abilities that were much lower. Almost all came from poor families. The women brought all kinds of sweet, gooey treats and little knickknacks for the children. Placing the treats on a table, the women moved to chairs along the wall. They made no contact with the children. They would never have picked a child up and held him or her on their laps. In fact, it was pretty plain that they didn't want the children's sticky fingers touching them. They sat there and whispered among themselves, talking about these poor afflicted children. They came once, and I wouldn't let them come again.

"But why," I was asked. They felt so sorry for those poor, retarded children. I didn't make excuses; I just said "No." You see, I couldn't have made them understand how their kind of sympathy was miles away from the kind of compassion Jesus taught. When Christ felt compassion, He entered into what the other person was feeling. He did not stand on the outside and point fingers.

Jesus' reaction was one of total acceptance. Look at the story Jesus told of the prodigal son. In the story, the father represents God—the God Jesus wanted people to really see and hear. In the story, the son is received back totally. There were no "ifs" or "buts" at all.

24

I'm accused of being naive because I keep believing there is always goodness to be found. I keep believing there is more potential for glory than for evil. Psychiatrists say human nature wants to believe the worst. Just as the disciples on the road to Emmaus failed to recognize Jesus, we fail to recognize the Spirit of Christ in the people we meet, especially if they are in some way different. I can never quite figure this out. I suspect it has to do with fear. The only way we can hold on to the wonderful picture we have of ourselves is to declare anything different from us as wrong. Somehow, if there is any validity in their being, then that takes away from mine.

We are also fearful of people or ideas that we don't understand. So we look for people's faults and never take time to search for their potential. You have to get close to a person to discover potential. All the "Yes buts" in the world are not going to make it right when we slam the door of prejudice by labeling and judging. That's how racism develops. There are many ways to practice racism.

When I was doing undergraduate work at Goshen College, I would ride my bicycle home at noon each day to get lunch for my boys. It was exactly one mile. If it was raining hard, I called a taxi. On one trip, the taxi driver ranted the whole way about black students at the college. At that point, Goshen was an all-white town.

I was so disgusted with what I was hearing I let him know how I was feeling. I said "Well, everyone has to have some one to look down on. So you look down on them, and I'll look down on you, and we will both be able to feel superior." I'm sure I didn't change his mind, but I cannot keep still when racist comments and words are being thrown around. You can imagine the conversations I got into when I was a pastor in the South for almost ten years.

To me racism is a creation of human ego, a creation made up of falsehoods. The name-calling that often goes with racism is sick. It is developed because of a need in the person who does the name-calling.

The Pharisees called Jesus names when they sneered at his home town of Nazareth. I doubt if we will ever get rid of such practices because release from our prejudices can be traumatic for us.

There is an unfortunate amount of warmth that comes from feeling superior to someone else. Lesser people exist only in the minds of those who need something to make themselves feel better. They don't exist in reality, and they certainly don't exist in God's mind.

Prejudice often also has to do with our view of jobs, especially menial jobs. It has to do with the treatment young people who aren't going to college sometimes get from those who are going. In the church sometimes we decide, in our smugness, that those outside the church are beneath us. In war the enemy is a lesser person—not worth anything so we kill the enemy. The Bible I read shatters these images. God keeps saying things like, "The first shall be last."

Going back to the idea of knowing who we are: when we do, it is pretty impossible for anyone to make us feel inferior or worthless. No one can make us into a victim unless we let him. If it's to be that way for us, we have to allow it to also be that way for those we meet—everyone. My dad used to tell me, "You are a child of God. It is not necessary to look up to anyone, but don't you look down on anyone either. They are also children of God."

As Christ's followers, we are not allowed the privilege of diminishing another's dignity, their stature, or their worth.

I listened recently to a young city councilman. He is also a strong fundamentalist Christian. His plan for making the city great was to shut out all those who deviate from being what he considered good people. I don't know exactly where all these people he deems unworthy should go.

For once, I didn't speak up. But if he does run for mayor, which he is thinking of doing, I will do my best to work against him.

I hear this same kind of talk in the church. Certain people don't fit, I hear others say. History has shown us all kinds of atrocities that Christians have practiced against those who are different in some way.

We can't let homosexuals in the church we say. People never forget that someone had a prison record. Someone makes a mistake and often they feel they can't be part of the group anymore. Clothing is important, more important than the people wearing it. Many of our young people, who are moving in a different kind of society, are made to feel the church is out of bounds.

I get hung up on all this, for one reason. I think the church is Christ's church, not ours, and I cannot imagine Jesus throwing anyone out, separating them from the place that is the very source of redemption for those who are being lost.

We forget that love eager to believe the best about someone is a redemptive force. We forget that Christ died for the lost. They may never know if, as Christ's representatives, we have no part with them. We forget that most of the people God chose to carry out tasks in the Bible had clay feet. Look at David. Look at Paul.

I like to ask people tied up in knots about homosexuality why they think God chose Michelangelo to paint the Sistine Chapel? Why he chose King James to transcribe the Bible into English? Both of these were tremendous acts of service to God. Some historians believe both these men were homosexual.

Jesus said "Let he who is without sin cast the first stone." That eliminates all stone throwing because none of us are without sin.

There are many ways to sin. Leviticus 18 gives a long list of sins. Homosexuality is one of them, but it is not given any more prominence than any other.

God does not have a hierarchy of sins with one being worse than others. So instead of accepting this, we pick a sin we personally do not indulge in and spend a lot of time really bombarding that sin and the people involved in it with all our righteous indignation.

"Yes, but we hear they are sinners," we say, "they are not like us."

Jesus said we are to love and forgive. Jesus was trying to show how God really is. If God had just wanted to be a God of judgment, Eden would have been all there was—no laws, no prophet, no covenant, no Christ, and no Holy Spirit.

I know as Christians we are a New Testament church, but I think we all ought to read the book of Hosea regularly. Hosea personified God's love. Hearing Hosea's message and acting on it is certain to label one as odd. Because, you see, you will love as God does, and that's not a common thing in this world. "Yes, but," they say, "you will be taken advantage of. People will play you for a sucker. You are going to get yourself killed."

I have a "Yes but" also. Yes, but the measure of how close we are to God can be identified by how much love we produce in the immediate world around us, including all those strange, unique people who are not like us.

3

The Haves and Have Nots

I SAT AND LISTENED LAST WEEK IN Sunday school to a vigorous discussion about people on welfare. The whole thing started because a Scripture in Proverbs about being a good neighbor led us to discuss Jesus' statement about loving God and loving our neighbor.

All the comments that came up were opinions that are always brought up. "I work hard. They [meaning people on welfare] won't work." A whole list of ways people cheat were brought up. "They have babies just to get checks" was a favorite theme. One young man said the government had no business handing out welfare checks. The practice should be stopped.

There were several who named some people who deserved help. I said three things and stayed pretty calm, but inwardly I was pretty disgusted.

One thing I reminded them about was the fact that if the welfare system ended, there would be thousands of middle class Americans who would be out of jobs. All those people at every level who administer the system would lose their own source of income.

The second thing I reminded them of was that there were many kinds of welfare besides that doled out to the poor (about 60 to 70 percent are women raising children alone). I told them that when I started college, I applied for and got government loans to help me. Then, because I went to teach mentally handicapped children in a depressed area, my loans were cancelled. That's welfare, I told them.

I reminded them that the field in front of the church sat unplanted for almost ten years while the farmer collected a farm subsidy. That's welfare, I said. There are many, many other subsidies—from houses to support of the arts. These are all money gifts from the government. These are all welfare.

The third thing I told them was that the government is taking care of the poor because the churches have stopped. If the church and its people were personally involved, cheating would stop because the relationship between "haves" and "have nots" would be close enough that cheating would not be possible.

For many years, I went to a large church filled with good people. When I would come with a need, someone always helped. That is, they helped with money. I could get people to help buy coal, clothing, and food. I could get them to pay electric bills or doctor bills. I could even get bail money if I needed it, but don't ask them to have personal contact.

"I'd help, but I don't know how to talk to those people." Personal contact is lost and soon interest is lost altogether, but the poor are still there so the government steps in. No matter how inefficient it is or how much money is wasted, the government program has to help. What else is there?

A few years ago, I saw an interesting set of statistics. If we help the poor through our taxes with government help, the percentages are that ninety percent of every dollar goes for administration and ten percent goes to the poor. With a lot of relief organizations, the percentages rise to at least fifty percent for the needy. In the church, at least in my church (the Church of the Brethren), the percentages are exactly opposite to the government. Ninety percent goes to the person in need and ten percent goes for administration. These are old statistics and may differ today, but I doubt if the ratio has changed.

What happens with the church? We know God wants us to have bountiful lives, but it's a little harder to remember we are to share that bounty. Instead, the idea becomes strong that if we have it, we must deserve it. If we don't have it, well, I guess we don't deserve it.

In conversations like this, I often remind others about Jesus' story of the rich man and Lazarus. Do we realize that in all of the New Testament, this rich man is the most uncompromisingly condemned? He wasn't necessarily a mean man. He let Lazarus lie at his gate. He let him pick up the scraps of food that fell from the table during his dinner parties. He never kicked him as he walked by. He let him stay there even though

Lazarus couldn't have been an appetizing sight with his body full of sores and the dogs licking them.

The rich man's sin seems to be that he simply never noticed Lazarus lying there starving to death. This man was present at the need of another and did nothing. That lack of response sent the rich man straight to hell.

Lazarus is with us. People are hungry, homeless, lonely, scared, and seeking. I believe there is judgment in store for those of us who will not let Christ remove the scales from our eyes and develop compassion for those in need who are around us. Pleading ignorance will not work. Remember the Lazarus story again. The rich man is concerned that his brothers will share the same fate as his. He asks that Lazarus be sent to warn them. His request is denied. He is told they have the Scriptures to warn them. That should be enough.

Amid boom times for some, millions more struggle financially. Many families are only a check or two away from disaster. When trouble comes, someone has to help. As followers of Christ, we are the logical ones to help because we watch Christ in action in our Scripture stories. We know how diligently he worked with the disenfranchised. He told us things like, "As you did it to the least of these, you did it to me." We need to say to each other, "Here I am, called, redeemed, healed, set apart to be God's gift to those around me."

Christ on the cross in the midst of all his suffering continued his mission of caring for others. He looked down at John and Mary, his mother. He gave them to each other. I believe that was the birthday of the church. That was Christ's final lesson while on earth. Take care of each other, that's your mission.

I used to get into big discussions in the South with other ministers. They accused my church of practicing humanism and said that we spent too much time and effort working with people's social needs. They insisted the work of the church was to save souls, nothing else mattered. They were wrong, you know. I know they were wrong because that's not the way Christ operated.

Jesus spent little time preaching. He did teach, however—always lessons about God's love. While he taught, he fed, healed, protected, and met every need presented to him.

I am proud of the fact that when Brethren missionaries go out, they do their teaching as they meet needs. They build hospitals and schools, dig wells, deliver animals for the Heifer Project, act as peacemakers, tend the sick, and do any other big or little job that needs to be done.

To have overmuch when there are those around us who have nothing isn't the way of a follower of Christ. The Scripture asks, "Can the love of God be in that person?"

4

The Church: Embodiment of Christ

To MANY PEOPLE, THE CHURCH TODAY seems irrelevant. Some never, ever, step foot inside its doors. Some drift in at Christmas and Easter. Some come pretty regularly with various degrees of commitment.

Even for those who do come, sometimes it seems only a habit or something respectable people do. In very few cases is the church the center of one's life anymore.

As a pastor, that's disappointing, but it is also understandable. There are so many, many things out there to grab our attention and sap our energy. We can see why the importance of the church ranks way down the totem pole in life's experiences.

For me there are reasons why church is an important part of my life. There are reasons that cause me to strive to get my family, my congregation, my friends, and all those people I constantly know who seem to have no interest at all involved in the church.

We need to go to church because Jesus did. Place after place in the Scripture, we read that when Jesus entered a town, he always went to the synagogue or temple. Christ, the perfect person, felt it was necessary to go. Isn't it logical to think if he needed the church, then we most definitely do?

We need to go to church to help build up the saints and, as one of the saints, to be built up ourselves. We can't be Christians by ourselves. We need the support and fellowship of others who share our beliefs. We all are bombarded constantly by other beliefs. We know Christ is with us, but it helps so much to be able to share deeply with a fellow believer.

We need to go primarily because our salvation rests in the founder of our church. How can we grow to be spiritually whole without the lessons we receive in church? "Yes, but," people say, "I can study the Bible on my own. I can pray by myself." Even as they say these things, they know they won't do them.

We have misconceptions about the church. A lot of people who have separated themselves from the church may think that those people in the church are too good, or they think they're too good, to associate with those who have left. What they don't realize is that true believers know they are sinners and also know they need all the help they can get.

Even we in the church get upset with each other. We expect the church to be without faults, forgetting it is made up of people—and no people are perfect. The church can't be all things to all people. If we love each other, we will make concessions for each other.

We have misconceptions about the role of the pastor and the role of the parishioner. My church believes in the priesthood of believers. As priests, we have responsibilities.

There is an example of this in a little story. The story says that most of us see the church as the preacher on stage, God in the wings prompting, and the congregation as the spectators. Instead, the story goes, it should be the congregation on stage, the pastor in the wings prompting, and God in the audience observing.

We need to have deeper appreciation for what the church is and has been. For one thing, we have to begin to see that each of us who takes on the name Christian and becomes part of the church, becomes a visible witness of the living presence of Christ Jesus. People look at us and say, "So that's the way a Christian acts."

We need to appreciate what the church has done. Almost every institution that has been built for human good in the world—colleges, hospitals, social agencies, and many others—had its beginning in the church.

The scriptural statements about sowing and reaping let us see clearly that, as members of Christ's church, the principle of sowing and reaping has powerful influences in the life of the church. We need to understand that as the body of Christ, we are always, every minute, every day, either sowing or reaping.

John 7:38 quotes Jesus as saying, "Whoever believes in me, streams of living water will pour out from his heart." It is not what we gain, but what we let

Christ pour through us. He doesn't shower us with blessings just to make us plump juicy grapes to be looked at. He wants us fully developed so he can squeeze the sweetness out of us, using us as a conduit to pass his love on to others.

People say to me that "The church doesn't apply to today's world." They say that church people are always pointing fingers. Church folks are forever passing judgment on people who are different in some way. People tell me that the church is like a lighthouse whose people are inside fixing up the place for themselves while desperate souls crash on the rocks outside. People say that the church is dull. We need faster music, more entertainment.

I have answers for all these things, plus many other detrimental remarks made about the church. But I have quit allowing these "Yes but" people to get me sidetracked in inconsequential things. I stick to what's important, so important that all the "Yes buts" in the world cannot even make a dent in it.

We all know there is a contrast between what the church is and what the church could be. I believe that gap comes in just a few areas. The primary one is that we have been inheritors of the faith, but almost totally ignore the fact that we must also be transmitters of the faith.

One way to be a transmitter for our Lord is with our tithes and offerings. We are called to be God's stewards. Our tithe is supposed to be given to the church. That's ten percent of our money. It's God's insurance policy to keep the church going.

In the book of Malachi, we read that if the tithe is not given, we are cheating God. Also in Malachi we are told to bring our tithes into the church. When we do, God will open the windows of heaven and pour out abundant blessings on us. You can't imagine how many "Yes buts" come up when the tithe is mentioned.

Money is just one area where we need to be stewards for God. We also need to tithe our time, our talents and skills, and everything we own and everything we are. Taking care of the tithe is a crucial part of the church and its people. There are other offerings we need to give for all kinds of good causes, but the tithe belongs to God and the church.

There is a second and even more critical part of the transmitter role. It was Jesus' last teaching before he ascended. We are to go into all our world telling of Jesus, bringing people into the church, and baptizing them.

There is a poem I shared with my congregation a couple of weeks ago that says it pretty clearly. Let me share it with you. The author is unknown.

> My friend, I stand in judgment now
> And feel that you are to blame some how.
> On earth, I walked with you day by day,
> And never did you point the way.
> You knew the Lord in truth and glory,
> But never did you tell the story.
> My knowledge then was very dim,

You could have led me safe to Him.
Though we lived together on the earth
You never talked to me of the second birth.
Now I stand this day condemned
Because you failed to mention Him.
You taught me things, that's true,
I called you friend and trusted you.
But now I learn that it's too late.
You could have kept me from this fate.
We walked by day and talked by night
And yet you showed me not the light.
You knew I'd never live on high.
Yes, I called you friend in life
And trusted you through joy and strife.
And yet on coming to the end,
I cannot now call you my friend.

As people of Christ's church, we need a loving concern for the unsaved around us. Let me finish this chapter with the story from 2 Kings, the sixth and seventh chapters. In the story, Syria has laid siege to the city of Samaria. It has gone on for a long time. People are starving. In chapter six, there is a list of some of the horrible things they are eating to stay alive.

Outside the city are four lepers. They too are starving, because even though they have been cast out, the people always brought them food. In desperation the lepers decide to go to the Syrian camp for help.

They know Syrians may well kill them. But they are dying anyway, so what difference does it make?

When they get to the camp, it is empty! God has made a loud noise, and the Syrians think a large army is coming. They run off, leaving everything.

The four lepers reap it all. They eat and eat. They carry off treasure and bury it, but then they begin to think of the starving Samaritans back in the city.

Listen to what they say to each other. "This is not right. We have good news. We have to go and tell the others." They do, finding the Samaritans hard to convince. Finally, the starving Samaritans go to see and their starvation ends.

There is a message for church people in this story. The lepers discovered a great wealth. They didn't have to share it but decided it was not right to keep it for themselves. We too have good news to share.

As people of Christ's church, we have been fed all our lives with the great feast that includes salvation and eternal life. We have this feast. We don't have to share it. We don't have to, that is, unless we remember Christ's commission. We know he says it's not right for us to keep for ourselves what the starving world needs.

It's hard to evangelize, to speak to others about deep, important things concerning Christ. I know all the "Yes buts." People don't want to listen. People will think you are a religious nut—pushy, crazy, and more.

Christ answers, "Yes, but you have to try." You can't let anyone be lost if there is any way in the world to prevent it. As the church, we have to try.

5

The Kingdom
of Heaven on Earth?

DURING THE YEARS WHEN I WAS pastor in Jacksonville, Florida, there was a men's clothing store that caused me a lot of concern. They sold a good grade of clothing for men who took big sizes. My husband liked to shop there until I persuaded him not to.

The thing that bothered me was a huge sign on their roof. You could see it as you drove the length of a main street on the west side of Jacksonville. I can't remember the exact wording, but the gist of it was, "God, take us away from this evil world. The whole world is rotten, take us away from it." I didn't believe that was true. I talked to the man in the store one time, but he had clogged ears. Wrapped in his self-righteousness, he could not hear a word I said.

I think the world God created is an absolutely wonderful place. Of course, I know there is evil in it, plenty of it. I know that Satan is very active, but I also know Christ said, "I have overcome the world."

The Bible begins with Eden—a garden, a beautiful home God meant for his children to live in. The Bible ends again with a garden in the Revelation—Eden regained.

Jesus taught us to pray, "Thy kingdom come, thy will be done, on earth as it is in heaven." I believe one of the things that phrase refers to is the breathtaking beauty of the world around us.

I have a backyard full of beauty. There are flowers of all kinds, big herb beds, a vegetable garden that produces and produces. Majestic trees are all around. There are all kinds of birds around the feeders—even pheasant. Deer, raccoon, and rabbits visit occasionally. It is truly a miniature Eden reproduced.

God showers us with so much beauty in every season, in the woods, at the seaside, in the mountains. How can anyone say the whole world is evil?

I once saw a banner hanging in a conservatory. The message written on it said, "The earth is crammed with heaven and every common bush afire with God. But only he who sees, takes off his shoes." At the bottom of the banner were these words, "The rest sit around and pluck blackberries and daub their faces, unaware."

Watching my granddaughters explore and discover, seeing their fascination with even the smallest bug, is a sight to behold. God is very much present in their wonderment even though some of their elders are telling them to put that nasty thing down before it bites them.

Recognizing heaven in God's created natural world adds so much to one's life, but there are others ways to discover heaven on earth.

The natural world is wonderful, but finding heaven on earth is even more wonderfully discovered in relationships. Each time we reach out in love to another person and that person feels God's love permeating them, that time and place become the kingdom of God on earth. Jesus demonstrated his deep relationship with all kinds of people.

There is an old German word, *Gewharsanheit*. It means the art of being aware. It means the same thing Jesus meant when he kept saying, "If you have eyes, see. If you have ears, listen."

It's the same thing Jesus meant when he talked about people having scales on their eyes. He was talking about the need for us to have a deep awareness of the people around us. "Yes but" so many say. "I don't want to be aware. To be aware makes me vulnerable. I don't have the time, the money, the energy to actually be interested in other people's lives. I have all I can do to take care of myself."

People seem to have a convenient shutoff valve. We only allow into our hearts and minds those things we think we can handle. Everything else is shut out. In a crowded place, we often shut out all the people around us, but let someone drop a coin, and everyone turns their heads at the sound. We hear and see what we want to hear and see.

Jesus taught us to pray that the kingdom of God would be as evident on earth as it is in heaven. We can be pretty sure of what that means because we had a living, breathing, walking, talking, in-the-flesh representative of that kingdom here on earth. Jesus showed us what the kingdom of God on earth would be like.

Let me share with you what my Bible tells me about this. Jesus was satisfied to serve. He lived among people as one who spoke for God; therefore, earthly things always came second. He constantly put more into life than he took out.

No wonder we hear the "Yes but" chorus at this point. People just don't think like that. People also have a hard time connecting with Jesus' gentleness with those in any kind of need or his courage in the face of hostility. Don't forget his impatience with rules and regulations, his integrity of spirit, and most of all don't forget the probing presence of love not even broken on the cross.

There in Jesus we see the haunting reality of what is real and what should be at the center of our baffling existence. There we also find God's kingdom on earth.

When we spend our lives wrapped up in hating, living in fear, trying always to get even, destroying in one way or another anybody who thinks differently, concentrating on self, blaming someone else for all our problems, always seeing everyone around us as the enemy, we are about as far outside the kingdom as we can get. We lose the kingdom often because we become befuddled by falsehood and misconceptions.

Television is a great weapon to build these misconceptions. Our minds play tricks on us. We tend to fix up the truth to make ourselves look better. Let me give you an example.

My son Jim, his daughter Jamie, and I went fishing on the Pigeon River. While we were sitting on the bank, a man came down hunting a new bait pail he had left behind the night before. He asked if we had seen it.

He looked along the river, cursing every step of the way about how the whole world was full of thieves, you couldn't trust anyone. On and on he raved and never once did he admit that he was to blame for leaving the new pail behind. He was attacking. His anger was a way of lying to himself. At that place and time, his anger shoved him right out of the kingdom.

When the kingdom happens in our lives, it does so because the spirit of God in me meets and reveres the spirit of God in you. When that happens, I will never try to gratify my needs over yours. I could never shirk my responsibility and pile an extra load on you. Looking at you, I could never do anything that would harm or diminish you or your worth because I know God dwells in you.

When you and I and our world finally learn what Christ taught, we will indeed be wise as serpents and gentle as doves. We will not steal, kill, bomb, imprison, or electrocute each other. We will have found Christ's kingdom on earth. Love will replace fear and justice will reign. God's kingdom will have come on earth.

Sometimes I want to say with the rest, "Yes, but that will never happen." Maybe not, but I know we have been given everything we need to bring it about. I know fear is forging the lock to keep us out, but I also know that love is the key to open the door of God's very kingdom here on earth.

Jesus walked this earth, showing us all the wild possibilities in the world that is not a closed system but a place alive with possibilities. The whole world is sacramental, my friends.

I looked the word *sacrament* up in the dictionary. It means, "Something regarded as having a sacred character with a deep mysterious meaning." We know the church has its official sacraments. My church has communion, complete with the love feast and foot washing. We have child dedications, baptisms, and anointing.

We practice these things of life using common elements to help us remember every part of our life as a church is sacramental. What is common to all sacraments is that they are moments when we are in touch with the love and power of God. If this is so, then think about these things—an embrace, ironing someone's shirt, a kiss, a gift of jellybeans from a five-year-old, a trip through the woods, planting a tree, a peace march, a coffee hour, a wedding, a funeral, bandaging a child's finger, psychological counseling, writing a letter, watching TV, talking on the telephone. Are these sacraments?

Was your answer no to some of these? Why was that? Did you feel that God wasn't acting in some of these places? The issue for each of us is always whether the universe is really alive with meaning or not. Is life sacramental (in touch with God) or do we grimly create our own meanings?

I believe a primary role of the church of Jesus Christ is to help us recognize the holiness of life, to help each other be in touch with the love and creativity of the maker of the universe, and to celebrate and integrate this into our own lives. In our cellophane-wrapped, rush, rush world, we spend so much time flirting with the unreal and the secondhand. Each of us needs help to discover what is real and most important.

We need to become real people, not plastic replicas of what God created to be the genuine article. We need to show we are created in God's image as people who care, who are not afraid to dream, who are not even afraid to hurt in our quest for Christ-likeness.

The church is not here just to impose on us rules to make us good (whatever that means). No, the church of Jesus Christ is to help us discover a God-given vision of a Spirit-filled world. This is a world where Christ is always present, in all creation, at a child's birth, whenever people find rapport, in a handshake, in an embrace, in every occasion of pain and joy, in all times in between. In every attempt we make, however feeble, to reach out to each other and our community, Christ's spirit is there, breaking into our lives, nudging us toward completeness and the kingdom of God on earth.

6

Women as Nurturers in Christ's Church

I WAS BORN AND RAISED Presbyterian and became Church of the Brethren when we moved to Indiana in 1949. I became a licensed minister in that church in the early 1960s. In that capacity, I served as Christian education director for twelve years. My primary interest in being licensed was to enable me to get into the jail more easily. But working in our church with children, youth, all areas of Christian education, counseling, planning, and carrying out special programs played an increasingly large part of my role.

I don't believe I experienced any "Yes buts" at that point. For one thing, all of that work for a very large church was done on a volunteer basis. When you do a large load of work for free, very few complaints come.

When my husband and I left to go into Brethren Volunteer Service, they hired a woman to take my place. I know she had many hassles, but I had left the state and didn't know the details.

I went to Florida as a licensed minister serving as a church camp director. While there, I preached in many of the district churches, promoting the camp program. The Winter Park Church in Florida asked me to consider being ordained. I already had the education so I made the choice to do that.

Only once while I was camp director did I feel constrained as a woman. The Fort Myers Church of the Brethren wanted me to come and present the camp program, but I had to speak from the pew. A woman in that church could not enter the pulpit area.

After I was ordained, suddenly all the Pauline Scriptures began to be thrown at me, a few times from Brethren Church members, but mostly from other church people in the South. The worst was after I began to serve as pastor in Jacksonville. The local ministerial society consisted of 150 male Southern Baptist preachers and me. I was either being called honey while the pastor patronized me with his arm around me, or I was being ignored and put down with remarks about a woman's place.

Some terrible abuse came after I started working with death row prisoners and was interviewed by newspapers or TV stations. My mail and telephone calls were full of hate messages. People would start out talking about the death row ministry but switch into tirades about a woman being a minister. Many times those against women in leadership consigned me to hell due to my role as a woman minister.

In the Church of the Brethren, women have been ordained for a long time. Women ministers are accepted for the most part, but there are still many churches even in our denomination that would not consider choosing a woman as pastor.

For all the "Yes buts" that still hang around in this area, I would like to explain how I answered people's questions in Jacksonville. The answers I came up with came out of the Scriptures and prayer. As a pacifist, my ability to calmly answer each rebuttal not only caused me to be able to function effectively in my role as a woman pastor, but also gave me all kinds of strength to initiate many ministries in the city itself.

The following is the grist I used as I milled out my position as God's minister. The word *church* means body of Christ, and since Christ was God on earth, the church is also the body of God. So then, what we are looking at are the nurturing characteristics of women in relationship to Christ, to God on earth.

We hear Christ speak of and demonstrate the role of a servant. This servant role follows the pattern of nurturing. This is a natural role for women. We are expected to fulfill that role in our families, and it carries over into the church. Women cook the fellowship meals, design the banners, teach the kids, manage the nursery, visit the sick, prepare the funeral dinners, sew the quilts, sing in the choir, play the organ, clean the kitchen, plant the flowers, take the minutes, get the family around on Sunday, and remind everyone in the family about each thing coming up at church. All these things are important; everyone knows that.

Ask any man in the church, they recognize the worth of all these things women do, but I wonder sometimes if we haven't slipped a cog in the purpose of our being. I wonder sometimes if we haven't pushed women of the church into Martha and her way of nurturing, losing Mary and her way altogether. I'm always reluctant to bring this up. If we ever lose Martha in the church, who in the world would do all that stuff?

I'd like to spend some time here as part of my "Yes but" thoughts introducing women who served God in the Old Testament and see what traits they had. Then I will also talk about women Christ related to in the New Testament and again look at the ways they nurtured the church and even Christ himself.

Let's begin with Sarah, long-suffering Sarah. She seems not to have batted an eye when Abraham decided to leave everything familiar and sure and go to some strange promised land. You remember all the things she went through, even being sold by her husband to save his own skin. Often we don't also remember that God wanted her to be mother of his great nation as much as he wanted Abraham to be father. More than once God had to get strict with Abraham to remind him of Sarah's value. Sarah was to be mother of Isaac, firstborn of Israel—which was founded by God's calling of Abraham and Sarah to be parents of God's chosen people. God tells them that from them will come a great nation, with as many people as sands of the sea. Isaac is first of that seed.

Then there was Miriam, a woman Micah was still talking about four centuries later. Miriam, who saved her baby brother Moses and was emissary to the people for Moses when he came to lead them out of Egypt. Miriam who was so loved by the thousands of Jews in the desert that they refused to move one inch in the march to the Promised Land until she was well enough to go with them.

There was Deborah, called the mother of Israel because people of every tribe came to her for advice. Barak even refused to go into battle unless she went with him to help direct the troops.

There was Esther, who laid her life on the line and went before the king to save her people. Her wisdom and courage saved thousands of Jews in the 127 provinces from India to Sudan ruled by King Xerxes.

There were Ruth and Naomi. Naomi taught Ruth about God in her household while they did dishes, made beds, and cooked meals. Even amid losing her husband and her sons, losing everything she had and returning to her homeland empty-handed, Naomi protected Ruth. When Ruth's baby was born, she placed the child in Naomi's arms. It was Naomi who would teach this child destined to become grandfather of King David and still later the ancestor of Jesus Christ.

There was Hannah, willing to give her long-prayed-for child into the service of the Lord.

Then there was Huldah. Huldah must have really been something. For many, many years under King

Mannaseh, anyone could be killed instantly for teaching about God. All religious books and everything connected with Israel's covenant with God had been destroyed. Mannaseh died and the boy king Josiah, came into power.

Not long after that, when the temple was being repaired, an old book was found. Josiah was ignorant of the law described in the book so he sent word to the people that he needed someone who could help him understand. Huldah was called.

All those years, she had kept alive the Word of God, preserving it until she could nurture it in the heart and mind of Josiah. She was instrumental in bringing about a complete revival of the people.

These were mighty roles these women filled. What did God see in them? What do we see? Courage stands out. You have to be strong to nurture. Think of Deborah in battle; of Esther before the king; and of Huldah, holding and protecting God's Word.

There was perseverance: Sarah and Hannah waiting for their babies. Naomi and Ruth trudging back to the land of Israel. There was love in every one of these women as they nurtured the Spirit of God in their time and place. Their skills are remarkable, and they didn't even have the living Christ as a personification back then as an example.

Do we fully appreciate all that was changed by Christ's coming? To begin with, do we realize that before Christ came, women couldn't belong to the family of God according to Jewish law? We became part of the family of God by forming a covenant with God. Men had to be circumcised to fulfill the covenant. This set women aside. They, of course, were not circumcised.

But in Christ, God changed that. A new covenant was made by baptism. Men and women could equally share in this covenant. With Christ's coming, we also see how much God trusted women. God the Father placed in the hands of a lowly peasant girl, a very young girl, the task of caring for, teaching, and bringing up the very Savior of the world—God's own son.

It was a continuing job. Mary is there when they take him to the temple at the beginning. She carries him to Egypt and back. She's there when he is lost in the temple at age twelve. She follows him when he's thronged by people and tries to get him to come home. She sees her neighbors almost throw him over the cliff when he visits Nazareth. She's there at the foot of the cross, and she's still there with the disciples at Pentecost. Mary moves from her role as mother of Jesus to that of a believer in Christ Jesus.

Jesus, God's son, also demonstrated his respect and trust for women. He trusted Mary and Martha. It was to their home he could go and relax. With Mary and Martha, he didn't have to constantly teach and heal. He didn't have to be the Messiah; he could just be a friend.

Jesus showed his respect for each of the women he met. Gently allaying the fears of the woman with a flow of blood, he called her daughter. He singled out a woman who had been an outcast for twelve years and gave her special healing. He listened when the uppity woman whose child possessed demons talked back to him. Refusing to be put off, she absolutely knew Jesus could help her even though she was from Canaan. Mark says that Jesus said, "O great is your faith, for this saying, your child is healed." Here Jesus seemed to indicate he was responding specifically to her argument. He endorsed her indomitable, snappy spirit.

Jesus' great sensitivity was especially evident when the woman accused of adultery was dragged before him by the sanctimonious men. Jewish law specified that, if a man had sex with an espoused woman, he had to pay the father or husband of the woman for making a harlot out of her. She was damaged goods now, you see.

The woman was not recompensed at all. In fact, if she was caught, she was stoned. The law admonished men but punished women. In Jesus' treatment of this case, he was saying women are persons, too, due the same process as men.

Jesus did not see this woman just as a disreputable sinner. He saw her as a person capable of straightening out her own life. He said, "Go and sin no more," leaving the choice in her hands and showing his respect for her ability to change her life.

Jesus always treated women as whole persons, treating them with high regard. All of which flew in the face of what was traditionally done.

Two women who illustrate Jesus' respect and appreciation for the worth of women are the woman at the Samaritan well and Mary Magdalene. These two women wipe out everyone of the "Yes but" put-downs aimed at women ministers. Look at what took place between them and our Lord. Jesus gave these two women two of the most important messages he had to give, and he sent them off to tell others, to repeat the message of Christ, to preach the gospel of Christ.

The woman at the Samaritan well was the first person Jesus told he was the Messiah. He had been traveling for three years with the disciples, but he hadn't told them.

After he told her, this woman who was rejected by her community had the courage to go back into that community to round up the people, to convince the people to come and meet Jesus. Her preaching was effective. She got results. Jesus stayed several days in that village. Many believed.

Mary Magdalene was the first person Jesus appeared to as the risen Christ. Peter and John had both been to the empty tomb, but Jesus did not appear to them. It was to Mary he came, giving her the message that, indeed, he had risen. He gave her the message and sent her off to tell others. He sent her off to preach the good news.

When people challenge me about being a woman minister, I might at times tell them some of what I have written here. For the most part, though, I just smile and remember all the wonderful ways God showed his appreciation of women, and the wonder of the ways Christ continued God's plan. The covenant I have with my Lord through baptism is my doorway through which I am free to become all I am capable of being. God gave me the gifts to preach and teach. What others think about it doesn't concern me very much.

7

The Gift of God's Peace

WHEN THE ANGELS CAME TO THE shepherds long ago at Bethlehem, they declared "on earth peace" and it seems like the whole world has been saying ever since, "Oh sure, tell us about it, where is this peace on earth?"

Where has it ever been? Those of us who are pacifists wonder too. Why are we chastised when we only seek what our Lord wants? We all know war drains us of everything from economic resources to spiritual worth.

We read articles such as the one General Dwight Eisenhower wrote. He said, "Every gun that is made, every warship launched, every rocket fired, signifies in the final sense, a theft from those who hunger and are not fed, those who are cold and not clothed. The world building and maintaining massive arms supply is not spending money alone. It is spending the sweat of its laborers, the genius of its scientists and the hope of its children. . . . This is not a way of life but a way of death. We are hanging humanity on an iron cross." He said all this in 1953. That cross today has nuclear weapons, chemical and germ warfare, and nerve gas at its base.

My church has always stood up for peacemaking. At least that has been our doctrine. Many Brethren have suffered severe persecution because of their stand against military involvement, whether training or fighting. Other groups of Brethren have not followed the church's position. On their own have practiced war on every level.

I think perhaps this comes about because we often start at the wrong end as we attempt to work for peace. I believe that war and all the hellish preparation for war are only symptoms of the peace that is lacking in each person. Big problems oftentimes begin with the shambles we create on personal levels.

What happens on our personal levels? Let me give you an example. I received a letter from a Navy chaplain I used to work with in Jacksonville, Florida. His letter said that he thought of me because this last year has been similar to the year I worked as pastor in Jacksonville. That year, 1980, there were several suicides on the base. There were devastating car wrecks with young sailors terribly hurt or killed. Almost all of them had to do with alcohol. There were way too many cases of wife and child abuse and divorces piled up all year.

The chaplain said 1997 had been just as bad. He ended his letter by saying he thinks these people give up too easily, that they lack the strength to persevere.

I would probably agree with him, but there is one point he is missing. If a person is to persevere, he or she has to have something to persevere with and for. There has to be some inner strength to pull from. A whole lot of people have only themselves to carry their loads. They don't have a clue about the availability of help from God. Worse yet are those who know about God and still don't have enough faith to do more than just practice lip service. Their religion is only skin deep.

We all at times slip out of our faith. Everything seems like a battle. Harsh words and actions take over. The storms of life inundate us. Wouldn't it be great if we could remember what our Lord did on a little ship on the Sea of Galilee about 2000 years ago? Wouldn't it be great if we were completely aware of his presence and had faith that he could say to our storms, "Peace, be still?" The storms in us would die down and peace and calm would be restored.

Just try to explain that to someone submerged in trouble. The "Yes buts" that come in such situations are usually filled with disbelief, snarled through clenched teeth that tell us we don't know what it's like to be in the place where they are. Try to tell someone submerged in trouble what Paul said in Romans 8:31-37. Try to tell them about God who loves them. Try to tell them that with Christ's spirit in them, nothing in this world can separate them from their loving God. If they live, they live in the Lord. If they die, they die in the Lord. Either way, they are completely safe. That kind of assurance brings peace, even the peace that passes understanding that the Scriptures tell us about.

The Jewish people who have always been involved in wars have always also yearned for peace. The peace they dream about is more than just the absence of killing and mayhem. Peace means a personal and social well being. They have a word that describes this. *shalom*. This word has deep meaning for them. It's a way of life that wraps their very souls in love, peace, and gratitude. They are searching for shalom.

I had great working relationships with a couple of Jewish rabbis in Jacksonville. We worked together at soup kitchens, at homeless shelters, and at the prison. We could talk, and one of the things I heard was why they were still waiting for the Messiah. They could not see Christ as that Messiah because they felt that when the Messiah came, there would be peace on earth. There was no way they could accept the idea that accepting Christ in your heart brought a peace far beyond anything found on this earth. They could not see that Jesus was the personification of shalom itself.

As we search for peace, we are usually trying to find relief from tribulation—whether it is war on a national scale, crime on a community scale, harsh words and fists on a personal scale. The peace we seek is linked with self-preservation. We see it with the Serbs, the Irish, the Israelis, the Arabs, but we see it also between labor and management, between the rich and the poor, between men and women, old and young.

Almost all the time our nation is half-deadlocked as Republicans and Democrats fight for position. We all talk about people having rights, but what we mean is that others have rights as long as they don't impinge on our own rights. That is exactly the opposite of the kind of peace that Christ taught about and demonstrated with his whole life. That peace comes with surrender and none of us are very good at that.

Alexander Mack, founder of the Church of the Brethren, once said, "Even though we are poles apart from someone else in our way of thinking, still we hold each other in love while we differ. If that happens, we may actually be able to learn from each other." That's a wonderful statement, and it seems to be one that is almost impossible to achieve. Almost all the times of persecution that have come to the Brethren, almost all the conflict I have been part of in my life, has come because it is so hard for human beings to allow someone else to feel differently about something. It always becomes a threat to us. If someone disagrees with us, then they must be saying we are wrong, even stupid, crazy, or something else that is detrimental.

The Brethren, if functioning as Brethren (and many never do), should have a vested interest in the following. First, we regard no one from a worldly point of view. People are not lumped into categories. We can't say all whites are a certain way or all teenagers are. Second, no one is seen as an enemy. Third, whenever we have contact with anyone, no matter how long, we need to recognize the spirit of Christ in that person. The other person should also see Christ's spirit in you.

They should be able to say, "I know who that person is: a son or a daughter of God." Every experience with every person has to come to a close in the attitude of love. If not, the persons involved are injured spiritually.

Real peacemaking is more than just believing in peace. Real peacemaking is finding a place to create wholeness in every person we meet.

I know why peacemaking causes so much resistance. There are thousands of "Yes buts" as you make an attempt. It's very difficult to even try to explain it. Often you are trying to confront evil with the power of love. It places you in a position to receive violence rather than inflict it. You have to do away with your desire to retaliate or get even. You have to do away with your desire to defeat or humiliate your opposition.

Not only external physical violence is avoided but internal violence of the spirit as well. You not only refuse to shoot or beat your opponent, but you also refuse to hate them. Booker T. Washington said, "Let no man pull you so low as to make you hate him."

Peacemaking calls for forgiveness. Jesus reminds us we have no right to seek forgiveness from God if we cannot forgive those who offend us.

For myself, when I can achieve it, being at peace comes when I remember who I am and whose I am. That's called owning oneself. When that happens, it is not necessary to scratch and fight to get ahead. You don't ever have to be intimidated or frightened by others. You don't have to impress others.

There is great relief in knowing that our worth is judged finally by God and not by our fellow human beings. When I start anything—I mean anything—I pray about it and put it in God's hands; then I do all I can. It's surprising how many things work out well and even if they don't, I'm still at peace because I know I've done all I can.

It's the same way with relationships. You constantly hold the other person up to God. Your prayers to God are for help so you can do or say the most helpful thing as you relate to the person. Again, you have done all you can. You cannot be buried in guilt or the other person's anger if the relationship doesn't work out, and they choose not to be at peace with you. Then it has to remain their problem.

There is not much anyone can do to you once you have found the peace that passes understanding. The peace the angels sang about the night Christ was born.

Conflict is all around us. As a person, I have to struggle to keep from being overcome by it. As a pastor, I find it almost impossible to teach Christ's lessons about peace because so few are able to hear. So few actually believe it is possible. But it has been possible at times and when it happens it is indeed beyond human understanding. It is indeed wonderful.

8

Death Row

I'M A PACIFIST. MY CHURCH IS ONE of the three historic peace churches. Being a pacifist means a number of things, but primarily it has to do with abstaining from violence. Most certainly, taking another one's life is not ever a possibility. That being the case, our church members are encouraged to choose alternate service over military service.

Also with all the hullabaloo about abortion, most Brethren would choose not to have an abortion. But then, there is the death penalty—executions performed by the state in each one of our names. All of a sudden, clear cut ideas about taking a life get a little hazy for many Brethren.

When I became Brethren pastor at the Jacksonville Church of the Brethren, there was no way I could shut out the fact that Florida's justice system was killing people as often as every three weeks in the death row electric chair. This was just forty miles from my church. It went against every basic Brethren belief I had.

More than that, even though the fundamentalist churches that surrounded me all believed it was the right thing to do, I still felt it was anti-Christian. How could it be right, or even make sense, to kill people to show that killing people was wrong? I had to be able to answer hundreds of strong Bible Belt Christians who not only approved, but also applauded the death penalty. For over eight years I collected, from every conceivable source, information about the death penalty. I continued this research when I came back to Indiana in 1984 and still do it today.

Using that collected information as background, I have worked in all kinds of ways to share why I don't believe in the death penalty. First, as a Christian, I don't believe Christ allows us to make that kind of judgment on another person. Now I know that there are Old Testament Scriptures that proclaim life can be taken, but if we follow those Scriptures, we are in trouble.

There we are told to kill those who sin sexually, those who use God's name in vain, and even those who sass their parents or treat them disrespectfully. In the New Testament, Christ did not say we should live out any such principles. Sometimes I think a lot of the religious community does not even know Christ came.

But even if I could put all my Christian faith aside, I still could not believe in the death penalty because of the awful discrepancies in the justice system. People, all kinds of people, argue with me. They say we have to have the death penalty because it is a deterrent. That's a lie. Other countries and about one-fourth of the states in the United States do not have the death penalty. These places have fewer violent crimes than states like Texas and Florida where executions happen constantly. States like Delaware that had the death penalty and then took it off the books had many fewer murders when the death penalty was off.

People say, "We want justice." What they mean is that they want vengeance. But if we speak of justice, when does justice begin? People screaming for justice should spend a few days with me hearing the horrible things that have happened in these inmates' lives. People should go with me to visit the homes and neighborhoods where these people grew up. I hope I would not resort to violence if those things happened to me, but I'm not sure I would have made it either.

Other arguments I get are that only the most heinous crimes end up on death row. This is another lie. It has nothing to do with the brutality of the crime. It only has to do with how much money the defendant has. When I left Florida, I turned over to the University of Florida at Gainesville records of all kinds of sentences handed out for very similar crimes. Some killers walked scot-free. Others got two years, five, twenty-five. Some got the death penalty.

The law very often uses plea-bargaining to arrange all sorts of deals. The sentence depends also on where the person lives, the color of skin of the person accused, and also the color of skin of the person that has been killed. If a black person kills a white person, the odds of the death penalty being imposed go up sharply. We have more than 20,000 murders in the United

States every year. Only 150 of those convicted of murder end up on death row.

The people disagreeing with me about the death penalty most often want to fight about money. It really galls them, they say, that their tax dollars are buying food and other necessities for convicted killers. They very seldom believe me when I tell them the facts about money. The truth is it is cheaper to keep a prisoner who was arrested at seventeen or eighteen in jail until they are very old than it is to give the person the death penalty and kill them.

One New York study estimated that New York spends 1.8 million dollars for a murder trial and one set of appeals. California revealed that it costs $4.5 million for each person executed in that state. Georgia, which pushes the death penalty, acknowledged that many counties in Georgia are spending seven times their annual budget to prosecute one case.

These things are what most people get riled about. One other thing I always make sure they hear is how many innocent people have been wrongly convicted. Since 1900, 343 people have been found innocent after spending time on death row. Twenty-five had been killed before their innocence was discovered. (For more on such issues, see the Herald Press book *Against the Death Penalty*, by Gardner Hanks.)

We have more than 2200 men, women, and children on death row awaiting execution. People say to me, "Shame on you for helping these horrible people."

I testified at a trial last spring and the young man's death sentence was overturned. That hit the front page of the newspaper four days in a row. A woman who lives close to me called every person in my church and demanded they make me apologize to the community. The church people backed me up for which I was grateful.

The prison system fights me every step of the way. I'm not allowed to take my Bible in when I visit the inmates. I'm not allowed to give them communion. I'm not allowed to baptize them, but I've gotten around that by asking for a cup of water from the guard after I'm in the visiting room. The men are then baptized by pouring.

I can visit these people. I can write to them. I can represent them to the prison. I'm always amazed that I have any influence, but I do. I don't get angry, but I don't go away, either.

Eventually the system has no choice but to deal with me. Probably the most important thing I do is reporting abuse and advocate against it until it stops. The guards used to tell the prisoners, "We can do anything we want to you. Nobody cares."

Now when something rotten happens on Indiana's death row, I'll get twenty or thirty letters right away. I've gone downstate to the commissioner's office a few times, but usually it's not necessary. Just the fact that I know and that I come to check up has ended a lot of the abuse.

Christ said, "As you do it to the least of these, you do it to me." I go to those that society has said are the least of these. I know that anytime you practice the kind of love for others that God practices, it is chancy. But it's also chancy not to practice that kind of love.

When we sit in sharp judgment and cut off the flow of God's love, we too will be held accountable. When there is an execution in our state, our hands are on that switch as citizens. That's a pretty chancy thing to be involved in.

"Yes but" I hear. "We want justice." Justice, of course, is defined as giving them just what they deserve. It seems as if we forget that if God operated that way, we would all be in big trouble.

Thomas Jefferson tried to stop the death penalty way back at the beginning of our nation's history. He said that no one is either good enough or smart enough to make that kind of judgment on another person.

The idea of forgiving persons on death row seems completely impossible. Forgiveness does not mean ignoring what they have done. Forgiveness has the power of transforming enemies into persons.

Matthew 5 says it all. Loving our enemies is the qualification we must have if we are going to be the children of God.

As humans it seems we feel better about ourselves when we have someone to look down on. We center in on people doing those sinful things that we don't do. People on death row are easy to look down on.

Again, we forget that God doesn't have a hierarchy of sins. No sin is worse than another in God's definition. We are simply told we are all sinners. Our only redemption is Christ's sacrifice, and the men and women on death row are offered the same redemption.

In 2 Corinthians 5:17-19, Paul tells us we have received God's justice and are reconciled to God. Now we must be instruments of God's justice in the world, letting others see that they too are eligible to receive God's justice.

Some prison officials have told me they resent me talking to these people about God. They aren't worth it, they say. The men are only pretending to be believers. That's pretty stupid, I think. What does it matter if by chance a man does try to fool me? We can't fool God, so what's the point?

I do not ask people on death row about their cases, but I know all about them because they tell me. I know about their dreams, about their fears. I know about their lives before and their prayers for the future.

These are people who have made big mistakes, but they are my friends and many of them are very young. Most I have known for eight, ten, fourteen years. There are no arguments in the world that will make me turn my back on these people—people who are loved by God just as I am.

It is an amazing thing when these people come to realize that God loves them. Few have any religious training at all. Almost none have ever had the opportunity to actually know Christ, even though they may have heard something about it somewhere, sometime. Almost always, their belief and trust in Christ begins simply because they trust me.

Working with a man as he prepares to die, seeing him grow from no faith, until at the end, he achieves peace is more than I can ever take in, especially as I stand by until the switch is pulled or the needle injected. It tears the heart out of me as I go through the last days and weeks with him.

At the end, God works a miracle for me too, as well as for the condemned man. We both achieve peace. We both know that what Christ said was true. If we live, we live in the Lord. If we die, we die in the Lord and either way, we are perfectly safe. After being through those moments several times, the chatter of "Yes buts" just doesn't matter at all.

9

God's Will: Absolute Wellness

This chapter mentions Monroe Miller. This whole book was written in honor of Monroe, my dear friend and mentor.

ONE OF THE PLACES MONROE and I are challenged the most is in the area of healing. There is a "Yes but" in the speech of practically everyone we know.

It seems to us that churches should be called health centers. In the house of God, we should be helping each other maintain wholeness in faith. This faith covers belief in all of Christ's teaching and actions.

My church, the Church of the Brethren, practices anointing for healing. This is done primarily for physical sickness first. There are also times when people are anointed for something that is causing suffering or stress in their lives. Examples include beginning a new job, moving to a new location, difficulties with another person, or a loss of some kind such as death or divorce.

Each time I anoint persons, I ask them, "Do you believe Christ healed people when he was present on this earth as a person?" The answer is always, "Yes." Then, I ask them, "Do you believe he has lost this power now?" The answer is always, "No." My response then is, "So then you believe that Christ can heal you?" That's when the positive answers begin to fade. Lots of times the "Yes buts" are strung out on the idea that, yes, God could, but it might not be his will.

Our response is that it is always God's will for us to be healed. God is love and love always wills wholeness. We ask, what parent would actually will a child to suffer, to be sick, to be in pain? Realizing that God loves his children far more than any human parent could, how can we ever imagine that it is God's will for any one of us to suffer? The things we blame God for would cause a person to be locked up in an institution if he or she actually did these things.

Someone is always standing by waiting to say that the worst kinds of things are God's will. Somehow, we can't quite accept the fact of God's absolute love. We also have lost touch with Christ's healing power and we have lost faith in its availability.

We believe God's children have the privilege of asking God for healing. We say exactly what we need to be healed from or when we are praying for someone else, we say exactly what is needed. Say it and expect to be answered. Expect it so much that you immediately thank God for the assured healing you will receive.

"Yes but," our friends say, "You can't tell God what to do." How can they think that? Don't they know

God wants us to be open and free in our conversations with him? He knows what's in our hearts anyway, why not be honest as we talk to God?

In 1 Peter we are told that it is by Christ's wounds that we are healed. With Christ's coming, this guarantee of healing comes. We are healed of sin, of fear, of doubt. Even the worst diseases, whether physical, mental, or emotional, lose their monster-like quality when wrapped in Christ-like love.

I think Jesus must look at us and ask, "Why are you afraid? Don't you remember I said, 'I have overcome the world, even the things that are plaguing you.'"

Genuine healing comes from the spirit of Christ in us. We are only whole in Christ when we are at peace. If we live, we live in the Lord. If we die, we die in the Lord, either way we are perfectly safe. "Yes but," the world says, "I don't want to even think about dying."

Monroe and I are well and able to do almost anything God puts in front of us. Monroe is eighty-three and I am seventy-four. People our age are not supposed to be this healthy.

When we say we believe our wellness comes because we ask God for it and believe it will come, many people take it as an indictment against them. We don't point fingers at others because of illness, but sometimes people seem to take it that way. Perhaps it really is because we want so much for them to give God a chance.

How many times have we heard, "You just wait, it will happen to you too." It seems not many really believe anymore that prayer brings healing. Maybe this is because we offer such inane prayers as, "God be with John or Mary." How foolish! God is always with each of us. It seems if healing doesn't come from a pill, a chemical, or a surgeon's knife, we feel it's not available.

Monroe and I have come to recognize the importance of these bodies of ours as temples of God, temples made in God's image, containing the divine spark of God-given life. This body is not just a body, but it houses God's spirit that dwells in us. We know God made our hearts beat before we even knew we had hearts.

We don't believe for a minute that sickness and afflictions are punishment from God, and we are startled every once in a while when we discover that idea is still around. Like Job's friends, there are still those who think a person must have done something wrong if disease comes their way. Great groups of very religious people are saying God sent the AIDS virus to punish homosexuals. It is hard for me to not speak out when I hear the God I love being maligned like that.

What causes illness? Well, for one thing, there is the way we care for our bodies. Poor diet, lack of exercise, not enough sleep. Everyone in their right mind knows we need vegetables and fruit, but many people won't touch a vegetable and not many fruits. Fast food restaurants, junk food, and almost anything coated with sugar is what is considered good. It's frustrating to try to cook a big family meal anymore.

Another reason for illnesses are the abuses people subject their bodies to—alcohol, drugs, reckless behavior, overeating. There are also emotional abuses—the things we do to each other, the easy way we use put-down remarks, the critical, judgmental way we deal with our world. The way we allow every fear in the book to take hold of us not only gives evidence of our lack of faith, but also plays havoc on our physical health. Holding hate in our hearts is like holding acid in our hands.

The medical profession tells us that stress is a big factor in all kinds of illnesses. Stress is often caused by the loss of something. Doctors say that one out of three in hospitals are there because of the loss-grief syndrome.

All of these things are the demons of today. But Jesus said, "In the world there is grief, but grieve not as some who have no hope." We have hope. We have Jesus. And the world says, "Yes, but Jesus never had to deal with the problems I have."

The world is full of the spiritual malignancies just mentioned as well as many others. These things, along with our strong bend to self-destruct, destroy our wholeness, our ability to be well. In Luke 9:1-2, Jesus sends his disciples out into the world to heal and to cast out demons. As people who belong to Christ's body, we too have the authority to cast out demons. But when we use it even for ourselves, we are looked at with suspicion and warned that we had better get help.

I want to share with you ways Monroe and I have found to stay healthy. Please remember, we are not declaring all these suggestions to be the way for everyone. However, we do believe that allowing Christ to be the great and primary physician in our lives is essential.

First of all, we believe all healing comes from God. Pastors, doctors, or pharmacists, all supply channels, but there is much more healing that comes from God than can flow through these channels.

Second, we maintain ownership of our own bodies, refusing to turn them over to the medical profession. Many people, who never would have something major done to their car without a second or even third opinion, turn their bodies over to doctors, allowing them to do anything they want. They allow their doctors to become God in charge of their future.

Because many of us are insured up to our teeth, it becomes easier and easier to allow more and more expensive procedures to be practiced on us. For some reason, we don't think we are paying if the insurance company foots the bill. We are paying, however, with the high cost of insurance, but also with side effects from the medical procedures. Monroe and I believe we are also paying with our souls when we have more faith in the practice of medicine than we have in Christ.

We go to the doctor on occasion. We take medicine as we decide we need it. That's part of the self-care we practice in appreciation for the wonderful gift we have received in our bodies. We also read, study, and learn all we can about other ways to take care of ourselves. We know about herbs, proper nutrition, control of negative thoughts. I practice meditation to relieve stress.

We both give ourselves, our whole selves, over to God. We have strong beliefs, first that God loves us and wants us well, and second, that God has made built-in remedies. The miracles of the human body are unbelievable—the way the immune system functions, the way messages are transmitted to the brain, what happens when a foreign object or bacteria enters the body and is attacked by white blood cells.

All the amazing functions of these bodies of ours are sometimes too much for a mere human mind to understand and believe. For example, how can we ever believe God wills sickness and pain to mutilate the wonderful creation of his beloved *children's* bodies? Knowing that God is able to create something that complete and that wonderful, why do we think God cannot heal it? The difference between the great storms and the great calms in our lives is great faith.

As a Brethren pastor, I have anointed many people as Brethren belief directs us to do. Many times as I have laid my hands on people and anointed them with oil, I have experienced healing; a few times, instantly. Always, I have sensed a great peace coming over the person as the healing process begins.

Not everyone became physically well, but even if the illness caused death, the peace and contentment remained. The person became whole in Christ.

For my own afflictions, I practice meditation. Using the word Jesus as I breathe in each breath, I release myself to Christ's care.

In his knowledge of how Satan attacks people of God, Monroe casts out his illnesses. In Christ's name, he casts them out. He's done this many times. Let me share with you a few examples.

One night Monroe woke full of pain. His chest and arms were in severe pain. He moved to his favorite chair. He prayed to the Lord. In the Lord's name, he refused to accept this attack. "Be gone," he said to Satan, "in Christ's name, I cast you out."

He almost gave up. Then at the point where he was about to call an ambulance, the pain stopped and it has never returned.

At another time when I had made the decision to leave the Senior Center and go back into the ministry, I really hurt my back lifting and pulling furniture. It was a very stressful time for me. I felt a strong call to go, but my seventy-two-year-old body was very reluctant to leave the security of the retirement center. The moving van was to come about four o'clock, and I went over to say good-by to Monroe.

Suddenly, I could not straighten up because my back hurt so badly. Monroe laid his hand on my shoulder and prayed, "God, Wanda has enough to handle right now. She can't carry it out hurting like this. In Christ's name, I cast out this pain." We talked awhile, and I went home.

One of the men from the church got there before the moving van and we sat and talked a while. When the van came and I stood up to greet the movers, the pain was gone. I could easily straighten up.

We believe that Christ healed people while he was here on earth. We believe that he has not lost that power, but that Christ's healing is still available.

We believe. All the "Yes buts" in the world are not going to change that.

10

We've Only
Just Begun:
A View on Death

THERE IS A SONG CALLED "We've Only Just Begun." I had arranged for it to be played at my husband's funeral. The words described what we felt after many years of sickness and several near death experiences.

Callie had cancer off and on for sixteen years. During that time we prayed, we studied, we listened to others, and we decided what we believed about dying.

We put together the funeral service that would be used for both of us. When Callie died, I preached his service, using the words we had carefully worked out together. It was important to do this, we felt, because it was a faith statement from us to the people there, especially for our two sons.

In the process of talking this through, Callie and I concluded that we had to believe everything taught to us about Jesus or we couldn't believe any of it. If we depended on Christ in our days of living, then we decided we could also depend on Christ in our days of dying.

As a pastor, I have been in the presence of death many times. For some people, fear is very much in control. Fear of the unknown, fear about whether they are good enough to reach heaven, fear of how the ones left behind will manage.

For others, it's more like anger. They aren't ready to go yet. There are things they still want to do, plans that haven't been carried out. The whole thing seems unfair.

For others, there may be a struggle at the beginning. Then as death comes closer, there is a sense of peace that comes over the person that is wonderful to behold. I've seen this happen in two very different situations.

One is the anointing service. Almost always when the person is anointed, this amazing peace settles on the person, in fact, on everyone in the room. Sometimes the person starts to get well immediately. Other times the body continues to die, but a sense of wholeness, wellness, contentment, and peace takes over and fills the person with a new kind of freedom—freedom that wipes away fear and fills that space with faith.

The other place where I have witnessed this is just before executions on death row. None of the men I have worked with walked those last steps filled with bitterness and hate.

Not all of these men were of the Christian faith, but all accepted my faith in Christ and in the God

Christ represented. I received some reprimands because I felt I could say to all of these men, God loves you and if you ask, he will forgive you for whatever took place in your life.

Some believed in Christ because I did, others discovered a deep relationship on their own. All of them reached a state of deep peace as the hour of their execution neared.

I haven't been challenged as often for my beliefs on death and dying as I have been about other things. Perhaps, this is because I have not been brave enough to pray openly that God take the suffering person home.

People resent that kind of a prayer, even though the suffering has gone on a long time, even though the person no longer knows anyone, even though the person is only kept alive by artificial means. It seems for all our talk of heaven, for all our talk of seeing Jesus face to face, we just don't quite believe it enough to want to go.

Those of us who are part of the church know the descriptions of what heaven will be like. The Bible tells us that we will be at peace. There will be no more sickness, sorrow, or death. Stories like Lazarus and the rich man tell us that we will be known as we are known, indicating we will recognize those that have gone before.

Jesus said, "I go to prepare a place for you in the many mansions of my father." He also said that where he is, we will be there also. We'll spend time with him. Other Scriptures talk about the thousands gathered around the throne of God, beautiful angelic choirs producing tremendous music, and streets of gold.

Perhaps the descriptions of splendor and riches are too much, moving it all into the realm of mystery and making it seem beyond what any of us would fit into. Angels have wings, but it doesn't seem that wings would be appropriate for the likes of me. Of course, there is a common belief that those who reach heaven will become angels, but the Bible seems to indicate that God has a set-apart group who are angels. These beings have always been angels, and we who are created a little lower than angels will share heaven with them but still remain who we are.

Things like streets of gold don't impress many people. In fact, for those who make any effort at living carefully without a show of wealth, it seems that gold smacks of greed. We'd prefer some of God's natural wonders like trees, grass, and flowers.

Of course, all of this is supposition. We don't know how it will be, and neither does anyone else. There are some things we do know.

We know we will be cared for. We know we will be safe. We know there will still be ways to serve God. We know that the place that Jesus has gone to prepare for each of us will be exactly the place that fits each of us.

As my husband lay dying for the last three weeks of his life, I sat by his side, holding his hand and saying over and over to him, "You are safe Callie, absolutely safe." He was unconscious most of that time, but he never let go of my hand. I believe neither one of us ever let go of our belief that, indeed, he was safe. Indeed, we both were.

It all hinged on our belief in Jesus. If we believe that Jesus died for our sins, that he was resurrected and lives again as God in heaven, that he also lives as the Holy Spirit in us, then we know nothing can separate us from the love of God. Nothing on this earth, nothing in the new life beyond.

That belief assures us that we will never die. As I have said several times before in these pages, "If we live, we live in the Lord. If we die, we die in the Lord, and either way, we are perfectly safe.

I want to end this chapter by including the words I said at Callie's funeral. These words will also be spoken at mine.

WORDS OF VICTORY

Callie and I want to share with you our thoughts about moving from this life to the new life. The Scriptures our son Jerry read shaped our thoughts. In John 8:51 we are told, "Whoever obeys my message will never die." In John 11:25 we read, "Whoever believes in me will live, even though he dies." We want to help you think what these words mean.

Do such words mean only that we shall rise in the last days? Surely not. Listen again to what Jesus told Martha. Martha had just said, "I know my brother will rise at the resurrection." But Jesus said to her, "Martha,

I am the resurrection and the life." And then Jesus showed her what he meant by restoring Lazarus to full life, right there, right then.

If that miracle meant anything, it means that those who die in faith will not taste death at all. There is only a change of place. They pass at once unchanged, only restored, and made whole, living, thinking, active beings.

So today, as I speak to you, sharing the assurances of how Callie and I believe, I want you to understand fully, I am not talking about death, but life.

How could I speak of death when the only thing that has died is just that part that hindered Callie, a poor sick body.

I speak of life. Life that means Callie has stepped forth in light. From weakness into strength. From pain into health and wholeness.

I speak of life because Callie can now see face to face, Christ, the Lord of life, and no longer has to accept him by faith.

I speak of life. Life that means Callie has now been given back his mother, his dad, gone so long, and his brother that he had lost and missed, but now can love again, not just from memory.

We're talking about life because as Christ received Callie, he will have given Callie the assurance that those of us left behind will be all right. That Christ is with us too. Callie can smile as he looks at his sons, knowing what good fathers they are. He can swell with pride as he looks at his beautiful granddaughters. He can see by the set of my jaw that the strength we shared for forty-seven years together has not diminished one iota, that his strength continues with me as I walk in the faith we shared.

Callie today has witnessed the love expressed by other family members and friends here as they applauded his life these last few weeks. He has heard the applause in cards, telephone calls, visits, and letters. Last Tuesday, he heard the additional applause as his Lord greeted him.

As Christ applauded his arrival, I know Callie heard him say, "Well done, good and faithful servant. Great are your rewards in heaven."

As you can see from that service, the song "We've Only Just Begun" was appropriate.

It is always appropriate in the life of a believer in Christ because when one has been promised eternal life, every point on life's walk is just a beginning. The point of death is just one point on that journey. It is of no more significance than any other point.

Each birthday, every new year, every high day like the birth of children, the marriage service, graduation, new relationships, all are places where we can say, "We've only just begun." But we need to remember, so is every new morning of our life, including that morning when we die and move into the place Christ prepared for us.

11

And Then There Is the Idea of Tolerance

I'VE HEARD FROM PEOPLE IN MY church who should know better that anything goes in the Church of the Brethren. They say there are no hard, fast rules, that concessions are made for anyone no matter what they are doing. Almost invariably such comments come from those who delight in pointing fingers and making harsh judgments, from those who rarely forgive another person's mistakes and think of themselves as flawless.

I've heard others advocate keeping certain people out of the church. I've heard them say they could never even speak to a professed homosexual. It makes them cringe, they say, even to be in the same room with someone who has AIDS, someone with a prison record, or someone who is alcoholic.

We as loving Brethren often do make concessions, knowing we are not to judge. Rather, we believe followers of Christ must continue to care for the person, to express love and concern even though we may not approve of the particular act they are doing. We stand by them. We let them see God's love by the way we love them. We always remember that although they are sinners, so are we. Our sin may be different, but it is there.

Let's look at how Christ interpreted this. When Peter first realized who Jesus really was, he was given strict orders not to tell. That was because Jesus wanted time to reinterpret the common idea of what the Messiah would be like. Jesus would spend his ministry letting people see the Messiah in terms of sacrifice, service, and love. He did that every day, all the way to the cross. In doing so, Jesus allowed us to see God as a heavenly father, who loves us, forgives us, accepts us, and never gives up on us.

Our roles are the same. As Christ's church, we cannot be that institution that busily stays to ourselves, fixing up our place while others crash on the rocks around us. If we recognize the spirit of God in each one, if we realize that each one is a creation of God and loved by God, it's pretty easy to be tolerant.

Not long ago in Sunday school, we got caught up in trying to define the word *goodness*. That word is a catch all. Through the ages, people have used this word as a gateway to the church.

We try to decide who is good enough to be called Christian. Conflict starts when we choose particular weaknesses of particular people and declare them bad. People choose whatever they are not guilty of and say it is bad. We have a much better guide than this.

The goodness of Christ is the real truth. All the nit-picking about what's right or wrong misses the point entirely. Every time we point fingers, sit in judgment, cast out or set aside other people, we have put aside truth, the truth of Christ.

When Christians begin spewing out hate they are acting just like Old Testament Pharisees. That is all completely outside Christ's point of view because Christians are supposed to be better than that. Remember when Christ spoke to his closest followers, when he began to teach the Sermon on the Mount, this is what he said, "Now I say to you, love your enemies, bless them who insult you, return goodness for hatred, pray for those who injure you."

Perhaps, we could avoid some confusion if we drew a distinction between liking and loving. Loving, as Jesus portrays it, has to do with good will. Liking has to do with good feeling. I don't really think Jesus was saying, "Feel good toward your enemies, toward those that insult you and hate you." That would be dishonest and probably impossible.

Suppose, instead, we defined the kind of love Jesus was talking about as a steady desire and sturdy effort directed toward the total well being of another. If someone is trying to do you in, you cannot be expected to cheer the person on. As a Christian, however, you are to will and work for what is best for the person.

There may even be times when you have to sacrifice for that person. We find out that often blessing our abusers is like a tiny crucifixion for us. Why are we called to such extraordinary behavior? Because we are children of God. Blessings, goodness, prayer, and sacrifice: these traits are expected of us because they are the characteristics of our Creator.

God makes the sun shine on the good and the bad alike. God sends the rain on the honest and the dishonest. Our panicky prayers in time of peril may betray our belief in such fairness, but that doesn't change its reality. Pious farmers receive no more rain than do farmers who are infidels.

All people are God's sons and daughters. We who know this have no responsible choice except to act like children of God. Jesus said, "My people are obliged to understand even if they are misunderstood. To comfort even if they are undercut." It was Jesus' purpose to push out beyond into circles of people who are different. For that reason, Jesus doesn't give us permission to be limited either by our prejudices or our preferences.

We sing of the wonderful grace of Jesus. The grace of Jesus has identifiable points. There's the grace of compassion. Compassion looks deep into the heart, suffers with and understands the need of the other person. Compassion ignores the unlovely and recognizes God's image even in unlikely places.

Another grace is courtesy. Courtesy is the art and desire to treat others with respect and understanding. It is politeness in the face of provocation—the turning of the other cheek when we have been offended. I'm appalled when we find in the church harsh acts of discourtesy. It reflects dishonor on the very name Christian.

Patience is also a Christian grace. Impatience has dimmed the witness of many Christians. We go around our world making all kinds of snap judgments about people we meet. We need patience to see how Christ is functioning in that person.

People are heavily inclined to lay down laws. We have never learned that you cannot legislate morality. No matter what law is enforced, someone will find a way to get around it. When Jesus gave us the Sermon on the Mount, he showed us that the law has limitations. The law emphasizes the deed and largely ignores the motive behind the deed.

For example, if we give to those who are destitute, that's a fine Christian thing to do. But if we do this while holding people with needs in contempt, then we are playing the role of the Pharisee and not that of the Christian.

Jesus' standards are different than ours. He would never allow us to say, "Church people do certain things. So to belong to a church, every person should do these things." Jesus would say, "God is good, but God will accept you while you are yet a long way off from that goodness."

The conviction that God accepts us, which is ours by faith, is the beginning of goodness, not the end. Such faith is very much like trust, betting our life that

God loves us, forgives us, and empowers us to live a good life. This is the exact opposite of legalism, which sees right relationships to God as the outcome of goodness.

This is why we're so quick to judge others. They may not have to be perfect to be accepted by God, but they sure must be perfect if we are going to tolerate them. We refuse to accept the fact that each one of us has a long way to go before we reach the standards of God.

The very fact that too many Christians refuse to tolerate others is evident that they too are a long way from Christ. We seem to believe that God has this category of sins. Some, those we do not commit, are at the top of the list. Others, those we do commit, are way down at the bottom, not crucial at all.

It's not that way, my friends. Jesus says we are all sinners, period. Christ had to die to save us just as he did for all those others. Galatians 3 tells us God shows no partiality.

I guess we shouldn't be surprised when people rail at us about our relationships, our concern for those who are outside the orbit of society. The same thing happened with Jesus. Someone was always criticizing Jesus for associating with tax collectors, prostitutes, and other sinners.

Maybe that's why people who profess to be Christians are so out of touch with Christ. We wall ourselves off from the very ones Jesus would seek out. We can't even find any tolerance in our hearts for the very ones Jesus would seek out. Jesus told us to accept the person where they are. God does.

In John 6:37 Jesus says, "I will never turn away anyone who comes to me." Jesus did not bombard people with overwhelming burdens of sin. He taught them as they were able to learn.

What is it then that makes being tolerant of those who are not as we think they should be so necessary? Paul tells us in 2 Corinthians 5:17-19 that we have received God's justice and are reconciled, now we must be instruments of God's justice in the world, letting others see that they too are eligible to receive God's justice.

Standing in harsh judgment is never going to show anyone the loving God Jesus taught us about. As we judge, we transmit to them our hateful meanness, disguised as the judgment of God. Many decide they want no part of such a God.

Sometimes, I have wished being Brethren wasn't so hard. Sometimes I have wished I could just accept God's justice for myself and shout with others, "Thank God I'm saved," while resting on my laurels until God calls me. I've gotten weary at times of trying to turn the world around. I've lost my courage at times when battles have raged large. I've been so disgusted at times that I have almost given up in despair. I hate always having to be the champion of some cause that other good Christians don't seem concerned about at all.

When I started working at the juvenile detention center as chaplain, I could not believe how justice was meted out. When I started working on death row, it was even worse. We have a completely unjust system. Whether one is found innocent or guilty totally depends on how much money the person has.

Whether it's working in the school system for children with special needs or with the poor in the community, I continually encounter the different levels of justice that pervade every part of society. There is no end to the battles one faces if one tries to level out the playing field even a little.

I had hoped that someday I would reach a time and place where battles would cease, and I could live in peace. But I can't find that place. I'm beginning to realize I'm not ever going to find that place. Even though I can't be glad about it, at least I feel grateful for the courage and strength I have been given for my role as a reconciler for God in my corner of the world.

The world tends to be our mirror reflecting back what we put in. Christ said, "What you sow, that shall you reap." A loving person lives in a loving world. A peaceful person lives in a peaceful world. A fearful person lives in a frightening world. An angry person creates havoc and anger. It comes back to us. Whatever we dish out, including intolerance, will come back to us.

Albert Schweitzer's philosophy has much to help us as we live surrounded by evils in our world. "No matter how great the evil in the world is, I never allow myself to get lost in brooding over it. I always hold firmly to the conviction that each one of us can do something to bring some portion of that evil to an end. And my prayer is, 'Lord, show me what I can do.'"

Evil cannot overcome as long as God's people oppose it. The first act of that Christ-like way is to love those persons that up until now, we haven't been able to tolerate.

12

Convictions
to Live By

IN THE PROCESS OF LIVING ALL these years, in the process of learning from people and experiences through those years, and in the revelations I have been privileged to receive, I have been blessed by God. I have achieved some certainties.

In this chapter, I want to try to list them. They are all areas that have produced the "Yes buts" in opposition to beliefs I hold dear. They are in no particular order but just listed as they have come to mind.

A few years back, Monroe introduced me to the author Oswald Chambers. Chambers was a great teacher and theologian who lived in the late 1800s. Today, people like Billy Graham and many other religious leaders quote from his writings.

Here is what Chambers says about this business of doubts and the constant questions about whether we are good enough.

> A pitiful, sickly kind of prayer and a selfish desire to be night with God are never found in

the New Testament. The fact that I am worrying about whether I am making it is actually a sign that I am rebelling against the atonement by the cross of Christ. We pray I will walk rightly with you, God, if you help me, but we can't make ourselves night with God. We can't make our lives perfect. I can only be right with God if I accept the sacrifice of the Lord Jesus Christ as my atonement as an absolute gift. There's a great deal of prayer by Christians that comes from actual disbelief. Jesus is not just beginning to save us, He already has saved us. Completely. It is an accomplished fact and it is an insult to Him to ask Him to do what He has already done.

Yes, that's what Chambers says. I completely accept what he says. It seems strange to me that so many Christians just cannot believe this at all. So many of us are hung up, believing in a standard of goodness. We either have done enough good things to get in or we have committed too many sins and are cast out. Will there be enough points, we ask, for me to make it into heaven?

Some Christians are filled with fear, others like the Amish say, "We have hope," but the absolute assurance that Chambers talks about is not there. It is as though we say, "God, you sent your son down here to be whipped, mocked, jeered at, stabbed, nailed to a tree. That wasn't necessary, God, at least not for me. I go to church, I pray, I read the Bible. I don't do any of those bad things you read about. See how good I am on my own."

I believe this is the great deception the church is playing on itself. It's the devil's theology from beginning to end. We are made acceptable by one thing alone, placing our trust in the life, death, and resurrection of Jesus.

A great many of the "Yes buts" come about because people of the church refuse to move from the Old Testament into the New. The Ten Commandments are the altar people want to bow down to.

We don't want to accept the fact stated in Galatians 2 and 3. The fact that depending on our salvation by obeying the law, the Ten Commandments, puts a curse on us. We simply cannot obey all of them all the time, and the Scripture says unless all the laws are obeyed all the time, we are cursed. Christ is our only solution. This is one conviction I definitely live by.

A second area of conflict is the fact that I see my role as an activist as a demonstration of my faith. Others sometimes pin the name liberal on me, and in some places liberalism is frowned on. Conservative Christians rise up in horror at the thought.

Long ago I discovered an amazing thing. If you believe what Jesus said about caring for those that are hurting and take one step in that direction, the scales literally fall off your eyes. You become aware of people and places in every direction that need you.

As I have moved out to do this, I can testify I feel the power of God at work as I actually practice my faith. I feel it in the strength of my backbone when I stand up to the prison system or social agencies for someone who needs help. I feel it in my hand when I touch a forehead with oil in an anointing service. In these ways and so many others, the power of God flows softly through me. This is very real for me. So real, in fact, that the "Yes buts" don't even penetrate.

The third area of convictions I hold is this business of deciding what God is doing or has done in our lives. Some of our fellow believers believe we should thank God for everything—pain, trouble, everything. Corrie ten Boom, who was imprisoned by the Nazis in Germany, belonged to such a church. The test came when she and her sister were placed with thousands of women in a huge, barn-like structure that was also filled with fleas. She couldn't thank God for the fleas because she couldn't bear having them crawl over her. But then she discovered that they were able to have Bible study with a tiny testament she had smuggled in because the guards stayed out of the building because of its fleas. Then she was able to thank God for fleas.

This is a wonderful true story, but it doesn't fit well with my reasoning. I believe that thanking God for bad things indicates we believe God sent them. I have little patience with those people who lay at God's door all the misfortunes of life. Everything that happens, no matter how heinous, there's always someone standing around waiting to say, "It's God's will." How can we do that if we know the loving God Jesus taught us about?

The fourth area of convictions I hold close to my heart is the one on wholeness. I believe that for all of us there is truth in the claim that we are only using a small part, a small percentage, of our physical, mental, social, and spiritual potential. James A. Harvard, a psychologist, said it more poetically. "Our fires are banked, our drafts are checked, and we are living on only a small percentage of our abilities."

Too many Christians are allowing themselves to die early to avoid the risk of really living to the full extent. They allow themselves to be embalmed in their own fears and are of no use on earth at all.

We never reach anywhere near the potential God has designed for each of us. We never even perceive the possibilities of wholeness in every part of our lives when we give God authority in every area.

We pray halfhearted, unbelieving, prayers, never believing all the Scriptures that tell us of the untold blessings our Lord has in store for us. We fill ourselves with pills and quotes from very earthly doctors and shut out completely all the healing available from God. We don't even appreciate or incorporate the miracles of self-healing, given by God and available in our own bodies.

We worry and fuss about thousands of things that sap our strength, confuse our minds, and destroy our bodies, absolutely refusing to develop our faith enough to give those things into God's hands. We forget that a big chunk of faith is courage.

If our faith is to be kept alive, we have to act on it in the face of fears and hesitations. Courage is one of God's gifts to us. We never seem to achieve any peace because we keep forgetting that God can even bring good things out of bad times.

Every area of our lives—mental, emotional, physical, and spiritual—is full of unclaimed potential. God waits and waits for his people to accept the key that will unleash the power to fix all those devastated areas of our world, allowing God's kingdom to come on earth.

The fifth area of my convictions follows the fourth closely. It's why I and others around me don't achieve that wholeness, that potential our Lord has for us.

I'm preaching about the book of Acts right now. Near the end of this book, Paul's conversation with the king is recorded. The king says, "Almost, Paul, thou persuadest me." It's where God's people often are, almost believers, almost Christians.

Almost is an empty word, without profit or advantage. What difference does it make if it almost rains during a drought? Can a person overcome fatigue by almost sleeping? A person almost persuaded to leave a burning building will still burn up.

A person who hears the gospel of Jesus and is almost persuaded to believe, still rejects God's love and mercy. One either reaps the harvest of salvation or one reaps the harvest of damnation. A near decision is no decision at all. To be almost saved is to be altogether lost.

Many have not grasped the idea that Christ must be Lord of all of our lives or he really is not Lord at all. So in large areas of our lives, we remain bogged down with worries and woes of daily life. We go through the motions of hearing the gospel, but it never quite sinks in and therefore we never manage to reap the harvest of joy that comes with being whole in Christ.

I believe those areas of our lives we don't give to Christ will be judged as addictions, as other gods we worship. Any area that is not aligned with God is never going to be empowered by the Holy Spirit. It will be outside the lordship of Jesus, and the harvest from those things will be very different than what is Christ centered.

My concept of hell is probably not acceptable to many. I feel the fire of hell begins to consume you any-time you are separated from God. All of us suffer such agonies in the parts of our lives we don't give to God. If then, at the time of our death, we have not achieved a oneness with God, then I believe that the fire of hell will burn in us with its misery for eternity.

The up side of all this is that the harvest of God's gifts are available to us in all areas of our lives. In amazement we discover that God doesn't judge us by our money or position in the community. He doesn't judge our looks. He doesn't even judge us by our problems. God sees the whole harvest of possibilities he has for us.

God isn't concerned with how well we do something. In fact, we are free to fail. What interests God are our intentions, our readiness, our openness, faithfulness, and love.

When we set aside parts of our lives from God, we become unable to say "Yes" to the opportunities God has for us. We live our lives deprived of the harvest meant for us. God's work goes undone. How strange it is that we call ourselves God's people and still grub our way through life with no more happiness and no more of God's power in our lives than the unbelievers around us.

I ask myself, and I ask all those "Yes but" people I know, "Why do we live lives filled with turmoil, desperation, and anxiety? Why do we only have small dribbles of peace, love, and happiness? Why is it that human beings are characterized by bickering and turmoil that makes the animal kingdom seem peaceful in comparison?"

Could it be that we are reaping this harvest because our consciousness is dominated by protecting ourselves, by panting about the here and now situations of our lives? It takes all our time and keeps us from even realizing what is offered to us by God.

Jesus said, "Put the kingdom first." He also said the most important thing is to love God with heart, soul, and mind and to love our neighbor as ourselves. Deciding not to or becoming so callous that we no longer have the ability to love as Christ taught us, triggers our emotions and we cannot perceive clearly what's real in life. We create horribly warped evaluations of the here and now based on our own un-Christ-like addictions and the un-Christ-like thoughts of the world. Setting Christ aside in any area of life warps our judgment.

The solution to all of this comes for me when I remember who I am.

I am a creation of God;
Loved by God as a loving Father;
Given salvation and eternal life by Christ;
Guided, comforted, and protected by the Holy
    Spirit;
Which dwells in me.

When I remember this, the "Yes buts" fade away, are only dimly heard, and become of no consequence at all.

The Author

WANDA CALLAHAN MARRIED Francis Callahan (Callie) in 1945. After their two sons went to school, Wanda earned a Goshen (Ind.) College degree in teaching and pursued graduate studies at St. Mary's College (Ind.) and Notre Dame University. She taught special education until her sons were grown, taking classes at the same time at Brethren and Mennonite seminaries.

Wanda and her husband entered Brethren Volunteer Service after their youngest son began college. Following BVS, she was called to pastor the Jacksonville (Fla.) Church of the Brethren, then Cedar Creek Church of the Brethren (Garrett, Ind.).

Wanda retired in 1986 to care for Callie. After his death from cancer at age seventy-two, she left a retirement community in response to a call to pastor the Wawaka (Ind.) Church of the Brethren. She has also long been pastor to men on Indiana's and Florida's death rows.

Roots of Wanda's *Straight Talk* go back to her western Pennsylvania birth into a privileged childhood. Her father was fifty-four, her mother forty-eight, and she had a bachelor brother at home who was thirty years her senior. These three people raised Wanda to believe she could do most anything.

From that home she moved with confidence into larger life. She was taught early to pray before you begin anything, then work as hard as you can at whatever you do. As she looks back over a life lived according to this principle, she is grateful for the results. Everything she has truly needed has come. She is convinced that never being made to feel inferior gave her the passion energizing this book, which is the concern never to make another feel inferior.